Ghostwriter

AF221102

Rachid Ferdinand

Ghostwriter

The Story

Short Story

»Ghostwriter«
Rachid Ferdinand

Bibliografische Information der Deutschen
Nationalbibliothek: Die Deutsche Nationalbibliothek
verzeichnet diese Publikation in der Deutschen
Nationalbibliografie; detaillierte bibliografische Daten sind
im Internet über dnb.dnb.de abrufbar.

© 2020 Rachid Ferdinand
Herstellung und Verlag:
BoD – Books on Demand, Norderstedt

ISBN: 978-3-7519-5306-1

I present to you…

…my Ghostwriter.

Contents

Ghostwriter – The Story

« He was born an artist in an artless mind. He was born in darkness and left behind. He is a Ghostwriter. »

\- Rachid Ferdinand

Ghostwriter

—

The Story

Inspiration

is not the thing that brings simplification in your own little

transfiguration or keep you save from stultifications in your

versifications. No, that's

Desperation.

Darkness all over his skin

I Still remember the first time I met him,
Darkness all over his skin,
He came to me, talked to me, told me he knew me, said to me:
"Hey homie, remember me?" I looked at him,
Darkness all over his skin,
Thought, who the hell are you? Why the fuck should I know
you? So, I said: "Get out of my way." And walked down the
street, put on my headphones, and listened to my shit. But
two minutes later I met him again, this man who's covered
with
Darkness all over his skin,
Thought, no way, it cannot be him. But he came to me, talked
to me, told me he knew me, said to me:
"Hey homie, remember me?"
I just walked away, didn't answer, what the hell could I have
answered? But then he yelled at me: "Man, I lived with you in
the mansard!" And for a second I was scared stiff, felt like he
just swift-kicked me in my fucking buttocks, and he was like:
"Shit, you know that you suck!"
Fuck yeah, that's when he got preachy, approached me, told
me he appreciates me but can't stand the fact that he needs
me, while I don't even know that I need him,
Darkness all over his skin,
And suddenly he just lost it, yelled at me as if he were actually

supposed to, and I felt like I actually deserved it, and he yelled at me: "You dumbass sucker, I'm the one who makes those motherfuckers remember you, read you, think of you, till they're sick of you, till they don't know if they should love or hate you, respect or discriminate you, bite or kiss you! Cause you, little prick, you would never be able to write shit like this! And you know why? Cause you've never felt like a piece of shit while the world pisses and shits on you and laughs at you! You've never been hated or discriminated against! Yeah, you're fucking right, the last one was Em's line, motherfucker! Your role model, right? Your fucking idol, right? Your inspiration, you think?! Your motivation, you think?! To be in his situation, you wished?! To feel all his desperation, you wished?! Thought it would have brought you simplification, in your own transfiguration or at least kept you safe from stultifications, in your versifications, DID YOU?!! Oh wait, didn't this shit sound like something YOU would write? Take a minute to think about who's the Wright of it. Ah, fuck it! I'm the Wright of it!! Oh wait, no, we're the Wright of it, right? Good, seems like you slowly start to understand what I'm tryna tell you. But you still don't want me, still wanna kill me, push me down the cliff and look back to be sure there's blood spreading out of me! Still wanna fight, still think you're right, still think you're White, still want apartheid!! But look at you, dumbass! Look at you, there's

Darkness all over YOUR skin!!"

Inspiration

is not the thing that brings simplification in your own little

transfiguration or keep you save from sultifications in your

versifications. No, that's

Desperation.

Yeah, lately the pen in my hand has been a little bit shaky...

Heading for that sacred knighthood.

Are you feeling or fearing love...?

Sometimes I'm drowning in my works,

sometimes I'm submerging in them...

One of my biggest fears?

Eyes full of tears.

There's nothing to do when your heart takes the lead.

To be safe from anguish,

That's all I wish...

Better to be a cipher than obsessed by success.

Better to be broken-hearted than heartless...

15

Holy Writ

And when we met, I bet he already knew how to get me into it, how to bring me through it, to make me feel I can't get it, make me feel I've lost it, fucked it up, messed it up, even felt like it wasn't quite my cup of tea anymore. Like it didn't belong to me anymore. Like all I've got couldn't score or even reach a four anymore.

Felt like he just spotted me, caught me, fought me, slashed and trashed me. Fuck! And since he hit me, talked to me, told me he knew me, said to me: "Hey homie, remember me?" I can't explain it, but I was really about to lose it, nearly threw a fit, but I didn't permit it. I still got to admit that there's something strange about it, almost special about it, something making me think he could actually fit. Could he really be my

Holy Writ?

Holy shit, how can I even think about him to fit?! Look at him, there's

Darkness all over his skin!

Man, I can't believe what just happened, how he just blackened me. How could he get that far, with that bizarre shit he's doing? How could I let him have so much impact on my writing? I mean, go back and reread this shit from the beginning and tell me I did not give him what he was heading for, made me unsure about this shit I adore. But don't worry, cause it needs way more, to make me burry and deplore the only thing I live for.

I guess I should rewrite it and take it back to the upcoming, convincing Arrandeth-Art and turn it into another unbelievable, lyrical miracle and raise it, like I usually do it, into a new

Holy Writ

But fuck, I can still hear him! Hear him laugh, waiting for me to do what he wants me to! Fuck you! Not for you, asshole! Maybe I overdo it, but I won't rewrite it! Cause I know that's what you're aiming at, trying to affect my self-confidence, but I'll never start having doubts in myself! So, don't even try it! My writing works perfectly and I know it! Just accept it, this shit's another

Holy Writ

Because I wrote it, so fuck it, I'm not going to rework it! There's no need for it! FUCK YOU!

Shit… Seems like I'm starting to get crazy, talking to someone I can't see, who can't hear me, who wouldn't even listen to me. But it's getting even more creepy because I feel that I'm losing myself, starting to have doubts in myself; leaving the way I used to be, losing what I wanted to be, even the pen in my hand is getting shaky. And I can already hear the real me, telling me: "Hey Arri, calm down, take it easy, lately you've been a little bit nasty, almost shady, and it's scary to see you leaving me." Yeah, I'm losing myself… But don't worry, I'll be back and bring you another

17

Holy Writ

I promise it. But first let's rewind this shit, in order to comprehend this emerging disorder in my writing and why my hand's shaking every time I hold the pen. What happened that frightened me so much when I met him, this man covered with

Darkness all over his skin?

Let me explain to you why I'm not able to do it anymore. Let me tell you the reason why I've lost it, why I can't make you feel it. Why I'm not able to write another

Holy Writ

Inspiration

is not the thing that brings simplification in your own little

transfiguration or keep you save from stultifications in your

versifications. No, that's

Desperation.

Yeah, lately the pen in my hand has been a little bit shaky...

Heading for that sacred knighthood.

Are you feeling or fearing love...?

Sometimes I'm drowning in my works,

sometimes I'm submerging in them...

One of my biggest fears?

Eyes full of tears.

There's nothing to do when your heart takes the lead.

To be safe from anguish.

That's all I wish...

Better to be a cipher than obsessed by success.

Better to be broken-hearted than heartless...

The Light

I already told you how I met him, this man covered with,

Darkness all over his skin

How he got preachy, approached me and yelled at me and
tried to convince me to think that he was me or at least a part
of me. Then he suddenly just disappeared, didn't go anywhere,
he was still there, somewhere. I could feel him, see him, every
time I looked at myself in the mirror, became unsure and tried
to figure out if I was about to lose my mind. Kinda crazy how
he got to me… But no, I'm not done, my run is not over,
otherwise I wouldn't be Arrandeth and as long as I breathe, I
will still fight, still write, till I find back the

Light

That guided me to where I am right now. People bow at my
work, treat me like a saint, even when I'm tainted and start to
act like a jerk. And sometimes I just want to tell them to stop
glorifying me, stop aggrandizing me. Fuck, guys, please don't
clap, it's a trap, it's crap. My works aren't that good, don't
forget, I'm still this dumb little guy from the neighborhood
who used to be misunderstood. Fuck, I'll come to no good!
And should I ever be able to receive that sacred knighthood, I
would still tell you to leave me, to let me, to forget about me
and to bring glory to yourself and find your own

Light

That might even shine brighter than mine. Trust me, you'll be fine.

But then there's this other side of me, this side I don't want to be. This side which tells me that this is my legacy, that people love me, they want me, they would die for me! Even God would take a bow in front of me! This other side full of haughtiness, bawdiness, obsessed by success. And I always tried to repress it, to suppress it, but fuck, I can't kill it! And all these years it was there, no HE was there! Even though I'm scared to admit it, but fuck, he is it! To hell with it! To hell with him! This man, covered with

Darkness all over his skin!

Fuck him!

Wait…, what was this? Jesus Christ, could it really be that he isn't it, but I'm it? No, I can't be it, that wouldn't fit, because if I was it, then I would quit. Maybe I'm really about to lose my mind. I need to find back the

Light

And remind myself that I'm the Wright. Yeah, I guess I'm going mental, please tell me I'm not crazy… And of course, he confused me with all this shit he told me. But the worst thing is that I know he's a part of me, he's inside of me! I already told you how lately my hands became a little bit shaky, but I didn't tell you how I started writing without even knowing that I held the pen in my hand. But no, I wasn't writing, He was writing! He was talking to me!

21

Let me show you what he wrote to me to confuse me and to make me think I've lost the

Light

Inspiration

is not the thing that brings simplification in your own little

transfiguration or keep you save from stultifications in your

versifications. No, that's

Desperation.

"Yeah, lately the pen in my hand has been a little bit shaky...

Heading for that sacred knighthood.

Are you feeling or fearing love…?

Sometimes I'm drowning in my works,

sometimes I'm submerging in them...

One of my biggest fears?

& yes full of tears.

There's nothing to do when your heart takes the lead.

To be safe from anguish.

That's all I wish...

Better to be a cipher than obsessed by success.

Better to be broken-hearted than heartless...

23

Remember

Hey dumbass, how are you? Yeah, I'm still there, deep inside of you and I know you're scared of taking a view, cause you fear that I could outdo you. And you know what? You're fucking right, I could do! Yeah, you know I could… Should I show you? No, there's no need for it, you already know I'm your

Holy Writ

But you don't want to admit it, do you? And you still don't wanna see that without me you wouldn't be who you are, you would never be this far. Even if you don't want me, dumbass prick, you need me! You still don't wanna believe me? Alright, then let me show it to you.

Remember

This time you hit the most powerful emotion that exists and you didn't have the vaguest notion if you could resist it or not, thought you've got to write about it in order to deal with it? But then you realized that your skills just vaporized into a brume, that filled your head with ignorance and not less with dissonance.

Remember

This time you realized you can't write about it, cause you're not able to wholeheartedly feel it? This time you realized that you're not able to write about Love…

Yeah you little genius, I know your weakness. Not only that, I

even know all your fucking secrets. Your lack of happiness!
Your fear of loneliness! Your fear of darkness! Your fear of
me, cause I'm your weakness! Well, actually I'm your
vigorousness, don't dare thinking I'm worthless. And yeah, I
witnessed those days when you struggled, puzzled about what
might be the reason for your fear of this simple emotion every
normal person can feel. Those days you puzzled about what
might be the reason for your emotional disaster.

Remember?

But you already know the answer, don't you? You already
know which one of us is feeling Love and which one is fearing
Love. You know which one of us is clever enough to sever
those perfidious bonds of Love and which one is dumb
enough to get under the thumb of Love.

Remember?!

Those sleepless nights you went through, felt helpless, didn't
have any clue what to do, after you got screwed up by this girl!

Remember!

How something deep inside you tried to keep you away from
her? Told you to forget about her? However, you still
preferred to give it a try on her! Well, how did it end up,
Mister? Oh, you fucked it up, lost her? Doesn't matter, just
forget about her and you'll feel better. What? You can't?
Fucker! Told ya she would tug at your heartstrings!? No, I
won't absolve you from your sins! I fucking warned you about
her!

25

Remember?!

Fucking warned you about this girl! Who was she again, what was her name? Oh yeah, now I

Remember

Wasn't it,

Reme...

Inspiration

is not the thing that brings simplification in your own little

transfiguration or keep you save from nullifications in your

versifications... No, that's

Desperation.

Yeah, lately the pen in my hand has been a little bit shaky...

Heading for that sacred knighthood.

Are you feeling or fearing love...?

Sometimes I'm drowning in my works,

sometimes I'm submerging in them...

One of my biggest fears?

Eyes full of tears.

There's nothing to do when your heart takes the lead.

To be safe from anguish,

That's all I wish...

Better to be a cipher than obsessed by success.

Better to be broken-hearted than heartless...

27

Suicide Pact

Oh, don't wanna answer me? Why not? Are you fearing me? Or just too good for me? Tryna ignore me? Don't you adore me? Want more of me? Just implore me, maybe I'll let you explore me. You fucking cunt! Who the hell do you think you are!? Arrandeth, the little bastard who mastered this shit like Escobar? Really think YOU've gone that far? Really think YOU've set the bar that high? Then why did you lose your way, when you heard me say: "Man, I lived with you in the mansard!" Yeah, what the hell could you have answered? You know, I actually read your

Holy Writ

Guess what? I had the same reactions as you on it. Saw all the contradictions and thought holy shit! There wasn't even a little bit you've admitted! Well, at least you owned up to your hands shaking as shit. But you still don't wanna accept it, don't you? Still don't wanna see that you need me! Guess if it were up to you, you would like to just agree to disagree… But no, fuckhead, I won't leave it be! See, if I let you get away with that, I would actually renege on our

Pact

In fact, neither of us is able to just say, fuck that. So, if you really wanna crack it, then you better listen to my shit! Throw a fit, if you want to. Just lose it, if you need to. But you better listen to what I'm telling you. Bitch, our

Pact

Is a

Suicide Pact!

Still don't react? Fuck, Arrandeth, we are on death! Your art's on death, cause I'm on death! Yeah Arrandeth, I'm dying, I'm evanescing, missing everything that made me keep on going. Missing this Arrandeth that kept me safe from death. And fuck yeah, sometimes I'm reminiscing about those days you used to talk to me, to be aware of me, to take care of me, instead of being scared of me. Reminiscing about those days we used to submerge in our works instead of drowning in them. But lately you're just stemming me, condemning me to be the bad guy, decrying me, like if you were vying with me to see which of us will back down first. The worst is, YOU actually created this

Suicide Pact

And trapped me into it! Fuck yeah, YOU wrote it! Don't believe me? Okay then, let's go together through it. Let's do it. Let me show you the shit you blew. Cause I don't think that you've got a clue what you did to get over the status of the ordinary Joe, do you? No? So here we go, here's how you became an extraordinary Joe. Yeah, just sit back and relax, here comes our

Suicide Pact

Inspiration is not the thing that brings amplification to your own life

...

One of my biggest fears?

Eyes full of tears.

...

Extraordinary Joe (1)

There once was a man standing on a bridge, listening to the murmur of the river, falling for the caressing of the wind. The stars were dancing over him, the dance of a peaceful silent night. At one end of the bridge, there was a city full of people drowning in a light-sea. At the other end there was a forest, cheerless, covered in darkness. And in the middle of the bridge, the man stood, quiescent, lost in his thoughts, looking almost innocent. Every beholder would have said he is sad, no beholder would have been wrong. But which of them would have sung along with him the song of being woebegone? His eyes were full of tears, wasn't that one of his biggest fears? But he just let them run down his cheeks, let them stream down to his lips, let them flow from his chin, oh what a sin…

The wind, playing like a music box, tasted those salty waterdrops. Wiped them away from his doleful face and whispered some words of solace:

"Dear blue Man lost in dolorousness, tell me, what took your happiness?"

The Man on the bridge was surprised by these words, which came from everywhere and nowhere. He thought it was absurd, he couldn't believe what he just heard. But didn't someone tell him about this magic bridge that brings the light to the darkness and the obscure to the bright, that could give you shelter and turn it all for the better, that gave the wind a wonderful voice and everyone a reason to rejoice?

"Oh, dear Mysterious Wonder, you shall know I'm a helpless lover. I'm beyond remedy, better not care about me…"

For a long time there was no answer. And just as the man thought it was all over, and looked up to those bright dancers, the voice appeared again.

"Oh, dear helpless lover, I'm really sorry about **Reme**. You might know there's a lot I can do, but I can't make a heart beat for you. Oh, dear helpless lover, I heard about **Reme** and You, and all the pain you went through. But why don't you just let her know, wouldn't it be better than to let her go?"

"Oh, dear Mysterious Wonder, don't you know? It's too late now for me to play beau."

"Well if it were so, then I would know it. But please tell me what happened."

"Oh, I wish something had happened…"

Stop it! Where the fuck did you get this!?

Shut up, shithead! I'm not finished yet! Sit down and let me write. Then we'll see, if you still wanna fight.

Fuck you! To hell with you!

Well, actually I was already there. It's pretty nice. Next time I'll take you with me, I promise it. Now shut the fuck up!

Inspiration

is not the thing that brings simplification in your own little

transfiguration or keep you save from stultifications in your

versifications. No, that's

Desperation.

Yeah, lately the pen in my hand has been a little bit shaky...

Heading for that sacred knighthood.

Are you feeling or fearing love...?

Sometimes I'm drowning in my works,

sometimes I'm submerging in them...

One of my biggest fears?

Eyes full of tears.

There's nothing to do when your heart takes the lead.

To be safe from anguish.

That's all I wish...

Better to be a cipher than obsessed by success.

Better to be broken-hearted than heartless...

33

Mister Nice Guy

"Oh, dear Mysterious Wonder, tell me…
What do you do, when your heart tells you "She's it. She's the one you've been looking for." And this, not in the way it did before, but so certainly and strongly and truthfully, that you know this time it's fucking right, and you can already feel how it begins to beat faster and faster and faster, until you don't know if it still beats or not?
What do you do, when your heart takes the lead, cause your mind can't deal with those eyes and those smiles and those laughs, and you know it would have fucked all this up?
And what do you do, when your heart tells you "C'mon now, do something, cause you cannot afford to lose her. No, you cannot. And you know she's worth it, and you know you need her, and you know you want her, so just show it to her!"
But I didn't do anything, cause I was scared…
Scared of what? Of losing her? How could I fucking lose someone I never had?! How could I dare think she belongs to me?! How could I dare think I belong to her?! How could I even fucking dare to start thinking, when I knew my mind was going to fuck up?!
Why did I even turn it on? Why couldn't I just let Mister Nice Guy, also known as my heart, deal with this beautiful situation he created? Why couldn't I just let him do his magical things and feel the beauty of love working on me…"

Inspiration

is not the thing that brings simplification in your own little

transfiguration or keep you save from stultifications in your

versifications. No, that's

Desperation.

Yeah, lately the pen in my hand has been a little bit shaky...

Heading for that sacred knighthood.

Are you feeling or fearing love...?

Sometimes I'm drowning in my works,

sometimes I'm submerging in them...

One of my biggest fears?

E yes full of tears.

There's nothing to do when your heart takes the lead.

To be safe from anguish,

That's all I wish...

Better to be a cipher than obsessed by success.

Better to be broken-hearted than heartless...

35

Extraordinary Joe (2)

The Man told all this with streaming eyes and a lacerated heart that cries. The magical everything and nothing listened to him, knowing that this Man was long lost, lorn and gone. There wasn't much that it could do for him, but there was still something. The timeless Mysterious Wonder had seen and heard a lot, had fulfilled lovely wishes and loony desires. But never did someone want what the helpless lover asked him for. The Mysterious Wonder became unsure. Should he really conjure this dark, dead-hearted Marvel?

"Oh, dear helpless lover, please be careful what you wish for. I know, your heart is sore. But you've got one wish and not one more."

"Oh, dear Mysterious Wonder, there's not much I want. Just let me forget her, her and all the others. I'm tired of crying rivers, tired of being a lover. Oh, dear Mysterious Wonder, just keep me safe from anguish, that's my only wish."

"Oh, dear helpless lover, you're riven by grief. It's no wonder you're asking for him. If this is your wish, so you should become the dead-hearted Riven and be safe from anguish. But keep in mind, you will tread this path together and one day, he's going to be more a foe than a brother. But you will have no other choice than accepting him as a part of you. That's all you got to do."

Suddenly, the wind died down, the stars stopped dancing and

the river became silent. The Mysterious Wonder was gone and took with him all the lover's feelings. Now the Man had nothing inside him and felt the darkness around him. He saw the world, how it was. Didn't like it, didn't hate it. But realized under which lies he was living. Under which lies we are living. He decided to tell it to everybody, to the world. He told them how it was, how it is, without joy, without grief, and the world disbelieved. It was too dark, too cruel for them. Still everybody liked his thought, all the things he wrote. It was something they never knew before, a view they never saw before, something new to explore, something new to adore. And that's how an ordinary Joe, a blue man, a helpless lover, became an

Extraordinary Joe

38

Your Ghostwriter

You dumbass Sucker!

Oh, yeah, that's better. C'mon dumbass, show me all your anger.

What the hell are you!? Fuck off, I don't need you!

Oh, really? You don't need me? Alright, then kill me. Do it. Kill the lunatic. Just kill this dumb little guy who makes your works illmatic and your fans addicted to your shit. Just kill me and let's see, who you gonna be.

Where did you get this? Who gave this to you?

C'mon Arrandeth, fuck, don't you get it? Of course, you get it, now just deal with it!

No! You're the evil in itself! You're not me, not even a part of me! Get out of me!

Oh, that's it, right? Yeah, I forgot, I'm the bad one, the evil one, and you're the good one, the one who does everything right. How did Em call someone like you again? Oh yeah, fucking do-gooder! Guess then I'm a do-badder, too bad I do better than you.

Stop talking shit you hypocrite. Why do you think you're better than me? Because the world pissed and shit on you? I guess it just did what it had to do.

Yeah, maybe you're right. Maybe it just did what it had to do. But what about you, Arrandeth? Did you do what you had to do?

What are you talking about? You know what, better keep it for you. It's surely just another flout.

Fuck, Arrandeth, I was always there for you. I did everything for you. I

39

was there when nobody gave a fuck about you! I was there for you, in your moments of weakness and loneliness. I was your wish, and yeah, I kept you safe from anguish. And there was only one thing you had to do, it was simply to accept me as a part of you! Damn it, Arrandeth, I saved you!

You saved me?! Really?! No, you killed me! You killed all I was! Yeah, now I **remember**. I **remember** what I wished for. And I also **remember** who I was before! But now I know, better to be a cipher than obsessed by success, better to be broken-hearted than heartless.

So what do you want from me now, Arrandeth? Tell me. Do you want me to leap to my death?

Just go away, I don't need you anymore. I don't want you anymore.

Oh yeah, I would go with pleasure, but don't forget, Arrandeth, we are bound forever. We'll meet death together.

No, we won't.

Sure we will. Arrandeth, we are one. If one of us leaves, the other's done.

Just go. You may be a part of me, but you're not me. I guess I must have a split personality.

Well, that's what you would like it to be, right? But you know there's much more than that behind me.

Then tell me, what are you?

I'm your desire, I'm your Ghostwriter.

My Ghostwriter? I don't need no Ghostwriter. Go, I'm sure without you I'll be better.

I guess you won't understand it and there might be nothing I can do about it. But we're bound for life and longer. Oh, dear helpless lover, we'll meet death together. I'll see you when our story ends.

Your Ghostwriter

...

...

...

Inspiration

is not the thing that brings simplification in your own little

transfiguration or keep you save from stultifications in your

versifications. No, that's

Desperation.

Yeah, lately the pen in my hand has been a little bit shaky…

Heading for that sacred knighthood.

Are you feeling or fearing love…?

Sometimes I'm drowning in my works,

sometimes I'm submerging in them…

One of my biggest fears?

Eyes full of tears.

There's nothing to do when your heart takes the lead.

To be safe from anguish,

That's all I wish…

Better to be a cipher than obsessed by success,

Better to be broken-hearted than heartless…

Thank you for reading…

We'll be back.